The Mouth
of the Earth

Manuel Rivas

The Mouth of the Earth

A boca da terra

translated from Galician
by Lorna Shaughnessy

Shearsman Books

First published in the United Kingdom in 2019 by
Shearsman Books
50 Westons Hill Drive
Emersons Green
BRISTOL
BS16 7DF

Shearsman Books Ltd Registered Office
30–31 St. James Place, Mangotsfield, Bristol BS16 9JB   *(this address not for correspondence)*

www.shearsman.com

ISBN 978-1-84861-623-3

A boca da terra was first published in Vigo in 2015
by Edicións Xerais de Galicia, S.A.

Cover photograph by Mary Owens.

ACKNOWLEDGEMENTS
Shearsman Books gratefully acknowledges the support of the *Secretaría Xeral de
Cultura, Consellería de Cultura, Educación e Ordenación Universitaria, Xunta de
Galicia* (General Secretary of Culture, Department of Culture, Education and
University Administration), in the publication of this volume.

'Endangered Tongue' and 'Saudade' were previously published in *Cyphers* magazine.

The translator would like to acknowledge and thank Leire Porral Combarros
who provided Galician language support, and Dr Mel Boland, Prof Diarmuid
Bradley and Begoña Sangrador Vegas for their soundings. This translation was
supported by the College of Arts, Social Sciences and Celtic Studies Research
Support Scheme, (National University of Ireland, Galway).

Contents

and III. FUNERAL ORATIONS

Hearing Things:
Tuning into Manuel Rivas's *The Mouth of the Earth*

Lorna Shaughnessy

For Manuel Rivas, words are the most sensitive of creatures. In the same way that frogs or glow-worms are the first to manifest signs of pollution in the natural environment, words suffer as a result of corruption in the sociopolitical sphere. In his work as journalist, writer of fiction, poetry or essays, Rivas is consistent in his role as custodian of all sensitive creatures; his writings document historical damage and alert us to potential future harm to our natural, linguistic and political ecosystems. With the same level of attention that a naturalist dedicates to minute indicators of change – the briefest of absences, the apparently insignificant break of behavioural patterns in a micro-environment – Rivas observes the signs and listens to the sounds that emerge from the mouth of earth. Like all his literary publications, this collection of poems was written in Galician, and first published in 2015 by the Galician language publishing house, Xerais, as *A boca da terra*. It represents another contribution by Rivas to the linguistic 'biodiversity' of Spain that he believes should be protected by policy-makers as a precious resource, rather than regarded as a problem.

The voices that emerge from *The Mouth of the Earth* are many and varied, and the three sections of the book reflect what they have to tell us in different ways. In the first, 'The Earth that Hides', we encounter nature as terra incognita. Mystery and enigma are central to Rivas's world view, and in their apprehension of nature these poems remind us of all we do not know, control or understand about the natural world that surrounds us. In the second section, 'The Ohio Scales', we observe the prints left behind by a wounded past and its wounded language; the *saudade* or yearning for lost meaning; the weight of dispossessed words balancing on the remembered shop scales of a Galician childhood. The final section, 'Funeral Orations', bears witness to lives cut tragically short through human injustice, but also celebrates the songs that sprout from the earth where they are buried, and above all, places trust in poetry's resilience.

The Mouth of the Earth challenges the reader to observe the world more closely, because it is precisely the things that are not immediately visible or audible that matter most in these disturbing times of endangered species, languages and histories. Invisibility has long been a concern of this poet. It is not uncommon for the reader of his poetry to experience a slow revelation of what was previously unseen, and simultaneously, a gradual disappearance of surface or assumed realities. One of his earlier poetry collections bears the title, *A desaparición da neve* (*The Disappearance of Snow*). We encounter immanent realities and unknown territories: a star that the night itself is not aware of; knowledge shared only between Jesus and Judas, like a secret joke; a poem that hides like a furtive creature inside the poet. Much of the earth that speaks to us here can only be glimpsed fleetingly, like the man who deserts the fog and is spotted through a train window, or the teardrop that evaporates in Antofagasta; or in the final poem, 'Singer and Minerva', that unique historical moment of cultural flowering and political hope that Galicia saw in the 1930s, truncated by the outbreak of the Civil War and the centralist policies of Franco's dictatorship. We discover that in both nature and history, the throbbing 'pain of the invisible' persists where injury has not been witnessed or has been forgotten. Such is its palpable presence in this book that 'History' is frequently capitalised by the poet. We repeatedly meet examples of a once visible past that has disappeared through human intervention, like the river Monelos that used to flow through the city of A Coruña, now channeled underground. However, in Rivas's world the disappeared and invisible are never wholly absent. Echoes of the past resonate through time and landscape, to a point where past and place become inseparable in 'Mother's Mountain'. Elsewhere, the equal weight and elusiveness of the past are captured in the delicate balancing mechanism of the 'Ohio' weighing scales. Rivas exposes the impossibility of quantifying the things that matter most, things that lie just beneath the surface, the non or not-quite manifest. Many of the poems poke fun at our absurd attempts to render them measurable, to weigh a lost sign of the zodiac or a strategic move in a game of chess; to parcel up a pinch of matured nothing, a kilo of hunger.

Rivas's poetry responds to the unseen by looking more closely at the wake of what has passed, or by peering long and hard into the fog of the present, ready to catch sight of what may emerge. Similarly, it responds to the inaudible by listening harder for sounds that may break through the surface noise of the present. Silence, for Rivas, can be either a blessing or a curse. It can indicate the presence of suppression and censorship, as in the poem 'The Mouth of the Earth', where the clay tells its part in the story of those buried in mass graves during and after the Spanish Civil War; or 'The Lovers', where lesbian school teachers cross the Atlantic disguised as a heterosexual married couple; or the story of how nuclear waste dumps were uncovered thanks to the courage and tenacity of a Galician skipper in

'Atlantic Trench'. But equally important are the positive silences of listening and reflection that we find in poems such as 'Inuit', where a woman's barely audible whispers can 'stitch a long, luminous and incomprehensible word', and the realisation in 'Man de Deus' that just as the lark hovers in the sky, suspended from its song, the poet hangs from his silence – temporarily airborne – at once still and in motion, steady and unfixed.

The 'Funeral Orations' that conclude the collection are this poet's response to historical silence. Rivas has described memory as a source of both nostalgia and future, and it has been a predominant theme in all his writing. Both his fiction and journalism have made significant contributions to sustaining the focus on 'historical memory' in public debate in Spain. These orations recover stories unsung by official histories. In the opening poem of the section, 'The Mouth of the Earth', the earth lends its voice to the project of recording tragic histories it did not choose to witness. In the second, 'The Gypsy Basketweavers', ghostly sounds of vibrating wicker rods resonate at the site where the gypsies were killed. Even the boots of a young insurgent have a chance to speak. These many voices remind us that the human capacity for cruelty and destruction can surpass our political and moral capacity to control it. They warn us against complacency and the danger of sleepwalking into an abyss, whether as a result of militarism, extreme nationalism or fear of 'the other'. They tell us that the consequences of poor political judgement in the past can have long-term effects for our political and natural environments. However, in their determination to listen to other voices and their particular form of ecological animism, these funeral orations are not without hope. There are many voices still to be heard, the book suggests, and many languages to learn before we can truly comprehend some of the recurring utterances picked up by Rivas's antennae, like the whinnying of absent or imagined horses, for example, or the trembling, stammering voice of 'a mother tongue at a bird's wake'. It is his desire to capture some of these barely perceptible voices that drives these poems to keep reaching for expression that goes beyond superficial explanation, to take the reader into areas of human experience where meaning appears not to coagulate or crystallise into familiar metaphor; experiences at times so traumatic they appear to defy expression. If one language will not fit the task, Rivas urges us to look to others, as these poems do, and strive to communicate in new ways, using the many tongues available to us through the mouth of the earth.

For my Crosswinds companions.

Wir Wandernde
Unsere Wege ziehen wir als Gepäck hinter uns her –
Mit einem Fetzen des Landes darin wir Rast hielten
Sind wir bekleidet –
Aus dem Kochtopf der Sprache, die wir unter Tränen erlernten,
Ernähren wir uns.

—Nelly Sachs, 'Chor der Wandernden' (1946)

We wanderers
Drag the path we have come like a suitcase behind us –
Dress
In a rag of the land we pause in –
Feed
From the stew-pot of language we learnt through our tears.

—Nelly Sachs, 'Chorus of the Wanderers' (1946)

I

THE EARTH THAT HIDES

Inda outra muita terra se te
esconde até venha tempo
de mostrar-se.

So much of the earth
still hides from you
until the time comes to reveal itself.

—Luis de Camões, *The Lusiads*

Restless Paradise

And now, night, go into town,
Find three more young men,
Carry back on your shoulders
The coffin of the moon
And from the earth that hides itself
Hear the whinnying
Of the untamed colours of horses.

The Man Who Deserted the Fog

Melancholy speed
That hides nothing of its past,
Land that peers
Through train windows
In search of the man who deserted the fog.

The Holy Tree

Mutilated tree,
Memory of the lightning-bolt
That killed then died,
Where ravens perch,
Blaspheming
With the hoarse echo of church bells.

Mother's Mountain

My mother left me
A piece of mountain
I've never been to see,
Always putting off
The day I would claim it.
But the unknown land
Cocks its ear to listen
And has a mouth,
Knows who I am,
Speaks to me.
They say it's nothing, really,
A bit of scrub
And an old pine,
Wounded,
That the lightning split.
So now I own
Some sky as well,
The wind's torn flesh
And a blazing flash
Buried,
Plunged head first
Into my plot
With angelic spite.
My inheritance thickens
To the sound
Of soldiers who passed
Through this corner of the globe,
Englishmen fleeing
From the French,
A wounded soldier
Drinking their warm blood,
Pilgrims who passed,
The hungry
Who gnawed on a log of shadow.

And those mute girls
Who stood,
Arms outstretched,
So birds could perch there.
All of it mine.
Mine and no-one else's.
They say it with a touch of scorn,
Yours,
All yours,
Night and day.
The land,
The split tree,
An angel's sword
Beneath a sea of thorns,
The murmur of history,
A spring of warm blood,
The whole world
The size of a reed-nest
Resting on the outstretched arm
Of a silent girl.
I've never been.
It's where I come from,
I carry it inside.
Hidden,
The land,
Inside
I hide.

Insurgent Nature

(Free Haikus)

The first clouds
Run in fright
Without stepping on the ashes.

Tree-boring beetles
Drill holes in death,
Coupling in the void.

The mountain smells of dead whale,
From its rotting beauty
An unnamed animal is born.

Like that martyr
Who stretched his skin
beyond the limits of his own body.

The first spider's web
Traps the drop
Where the dawn trembles.

Objects recoil in horror
When a man
Raises his hand against himself.

On the football pitch
A mole
Has parodied the centre circle.

The animist stupor
Of domestic appliances
That cannot be repaired.

The apostate rancour
Of tractors
On abandoned farms.

In the hidden earth
Words dig deep
Face up.

The slug traces
A sparkling chasm
To the sound of light.

The absolute sea explodes
In the place where infinity
Fishes with dynamite.

A high wind
Fills the ruins
With motionless life.

Silence falls quiet
To watch
A thousand years of laughter pass by.

Vegetation
Hides out in the house,
Guards the path.

Forgetfulness hunts
In time's meadows
With a ferret in its pocket.

A black shadow
Fled from the poem
Along the fossil-line of the horizon.

The purple of the heather
Nourishes
The fasting earth.

Thorns in the whin bush
Pin flowers to the headstone
Of an ancient sky.

Fermenting nettles,
White, bewitched
Shadow.

Can you hear crippled memory
With its wooden leg
on the staircase of light?

Night gnaws at the gums
Of absences
The moon brings to light.

A deep path
And a hidden body
In a vagabond soul.

All night, the phalaena moth
Fought with the light
To see in the dark of day.

The mystery of the wound
Is in the precision of the scar,
An ideogram on the skin.

The full moon
Is on the lookout
For unread ruins.

A strange word
Allowed itself to be written
Without feeling any fear.

Monelos

At night,
Sleepwalking trees
Stalk the missing river.

Throb

That humming in the oak trees
Is the pain of the invisible
at not being seen.

Praza das Bárbaras

Leaves that fall in the night,
Self-absorbed
As the accidents of love.

Resurrection

Climb to the summit of Pindo
On an Easter Sunday,
Pealing underwater bells at your back.

Mount Pindo,
Not a trace of death
On your remains.

The stones are in the places
They want to be.
Or are they clouds that gather
Where they want to meet?

Soesto

Along the high grasses
Of the hillside
An amphibious cloud,
Salamander shadow,
Pants.
The stream takes cover
In the calyx of a flower
With a thousand years of laughter.
Down in the dunes
Amongst the sea-thistles,
Wonder advances
From the line of the horizon.
Everything crouches in wait
For a storm of butterflies.

On Man de Deus

The lark hangs,
Suspended from its song.
I hang from my silence,
Listen to the hymn
That questions fate
Like the Hosanna
In the wind's youth.
But if I kneel,
Everything will come crashing down.

Dada in the Tree-Tops

The wind sways the branches
Like a good death.
Leaves from the apple tree
Break away from History,
Acrobats in free-fall
That cling to the shirt-tails of souls,
Sparks in the half-light
Of dusk
On the plain.

Certified Shipwrecked

For Haroldo Conti, who proudly
presented the certificate that said
he had been shipwrecked.

The wave will not roll back from its course.
It knows its best self
Lies on the surf break
Of History.
Conscience is a question of style:
Never cheat in defeat.
Fall with dignity
From the Horizon-Line
Like the first man shipwrecked
On the first sea.

Blackbird

Drunk on the fruit of the strawberry tree,
The blackbird pecks
At a star
That the night itself
Didn't know was there.

The Winds of Traba

Wind that blows from Traba,
Hay, fern and fennel,
Every thing flocks
Whispers, lows, howls,
Every thing flocks.

Wind that blows from Traba,
Umbellate spray,
Yarrow-flower sea,
Wind-frayed paths.
A gust of jellyfish in the grass,
Every thing flocks.

Everything shudders,
Everything stutters,
Like a mother tongue
At a bird's wake.

Collision

The animal groaned
Prophesies of pain
That made it an unappealing victim.

Wax Dolls (Fumaria Muralis)

The raw pink of wax dolls,
Suicidal beauty of the species
On hostile summer asphalt.

Sabucedo

This year again
The mare-herd emerges from the invisible,
Biting their own breath.
The men believe they have found them,
Their covetous eyes
Drilling into the fog.
Their own shouts
A whinnying of horses
Not yet born.
The men,
Like wolves of laughter,
Follow the herd
Towards the town and the enclosure.
In the first ring,
In a convex sea of eyes,
The tamers leap
Onto history's back
To cut the manes of the wind;
Their bloody saliva
a bookplate on the ground.
The men
Are the thing
The horses dreamed.

Murmurings

In the hidden earth
A language is spoken
That rains in its bare feet.

Situationist Rondel

Sea pinks charm
Stirring the wind that
Shakes the sea pinks
Where the ninth wave
Moves the sea
A cliff-top gaze
Dies in the depths
And before dying stirs
The sea pinks' charm.

Hallelujah

Eyes have a memory that smells,
The flurry of putrid light
In the pigeon loft.

Sleepless

The full moon
Tenons
Words.

Tubers
With the bulging eyes
Of a black sun.

Fear spawns
Invasive species
At the root of the impenetrable.

The Curve

The worst wound
Is cut in a straight line.
Observe the great scar of the horizon.
The earth crowns
From beyond Cézanne's curve.
You can squint all you want,
But it's the earth that sees.

II

THE OHIO SCALES

Ti vas cun saco de sombras ó lombo.

You set off with a sack of shadows on your back.

LUIS PIMENTEL

From *Sombra do aire na herba*
(*The Shadow of Wind in the Grass*)

The Weighing Scales

The needle always trembled
For some reason.
Like a new fear,
The Ohio Scales
Always jumped a few grams ahead,
The weight of a rind of emptiness
Or a breeze from the west,
The Ohio Scales,
Or the weight of a soul
On the white counter,
The Ohio Scales,
That fixed stare
On a scoop of flour,
A handful of sugar,
A measure of salt,
Or on the strip of lard
Unhooked from the ceiling
By the shop assistant,
The inescapable
Weight
Of a lost sign
Of the zodiac.

The Coin

For Teresa Alvajar

We were in Leonor's shop.
Without her realising,
The customer with the hoarse voice,
Black blouse,
And the arms of a woman
Widowed by a living man,
Had dropped a coin on the ground.
I covered it with my foot.
When she went to pay
It couldn't be found.
Round and round she went,
Searching all around me,
Inconsolable,
Round and round again
Till I felt the pulse
Of a straitened planet,
Disoriented,
Round and round,
And the coin was feeling it too,
I could sense its palpitations beneath my foot,
But I stood there, rigid,
Eyes fixed
On the tip of the arrow
Of the Ohio Scales.

The Errand

What will you have today, young man?
I'll have a slow sinking feeling
Please
And a slice of salted horizon.
Give me
A handful of dry eyes
Without the tear-fat.
And while you're there, I'll have a touch of nothing.
Just a pinch of extra mature nothing.

Endangered Tongue

The mouths of post-boxes
Ruminating
On the sociology of absences.
The sparrow pecking
At disappointed onomatopoeias
Among the losing tickets
Of the charity Tombola.
The one-eyed light
like an insect informer
in the room of a boarding house.
The sound of eddies
Against the sash windows
Of an underwater tavern.
The timbre of a blind man's cane
In the awkward angles
Of street corners.
The precision of place names
At the scene of an accident.
The indescribable sigh
Of nomadic love
Beyond Cézanne's curve.
Laughter
At the foot of the gallows.
I'll have a kilo of hunger
Today, please,
A litre of thirst,
And a slice of endangered tongue.

Celtic Apocalypse

While you're at it
Pour me a good shot of Apocalypse,
A dram that would topple a god,
A Raging Tiger absinthe
Distilled in wormwood.
I want to see the woods advancing
At night,
Hear the loud breathing of people in the undergrowth
Chewing on the berries of creepers,
Digging up curses where a tooth aches.
The flight from
Unreal reality
Filmed as fiction
By a neurotic god,
Meticulous and stubborn
As the tourist's
Steaming shadow,
His acrylic footprint,
His vampire kit,
On the path to the site
Of archaeological beauty.

Spiritual Exercise

When the time comes,
Will I be able to take the weight
Of my own death, a death
Paralysed by incomprehension?

Will I be strong enough
To tie up my soul
Like a storm
With a sailor's knot?

Will I be able to stay quiet
In the presence of the Supreme Being,
Wrong-foot him with my silence?
As Levi said: what is God's silence
In the face of the silence of Man?

Guilt in a Time of Crisis

On the sea wall
The fisherman's pose
As he sat apart
Propped up by his line
Resting against a float
And flaying
His soul on the hook
Almost painted
A self-portrait
A harbour scene in oils
A hypnotic sadness
Braiding land and sea
Until my father
Poseidon
Pulled me away:

That's the man
Who drove all the squid
From the shores of Galicia!

Breaking News

As surely as Oedipus annihilated
The creature with the curving claws,
The singer of enigmas,
The news is broken.

Saudade

There was once a whore called Saudade
Who walked the river-bank
In Porto
In her high heels
Like a woman walking barefoot.
The same fog that protected her
killed her.
Her tongue, sharp
As a barber's blade,
Called out to the poet:
Here she is, your Saudade,
Sacred nostalgia
And hunger for the future.
The jibe
Stumbled like an ugly laugh,
And the echo of her high heels
Sent back
The bare percussion of the truth.

O'Clock

Travellers unload their bodies
Sideways
Advance
Like a winter offensive
Scourging their shadows
With the relentless nostalgia
Of endangered
Celluloid.

The Wound in the Sphere

I'll never forget you, May 8th 2010.
Officially declared Day of Sadness.
In the football league
Barça and Madrid both won.
People were happy,
They would've been even happier
If they'd known
This was the saddest day ever.
In the Concert Hall
the Donostiarra choir
Sang Giuseppe Verdi's 'Requiem'
Like never before,
But the voice of the evening,
Take note of the name,
Was mezzo Anna Smirnova.
Everyone was applauded,
Perhaps a little too much
As is often the case with classical ovations.
Or perhaps some were in on the secret.
Lots of civil servants were there,
The odd Police Inspector.
Watchmakers too.
But it was one of the musicians,
The percussionist on timpani,
Who must have suspected something;
For in a moment of silence
He placed his ear to the wound in the sphere.

Introduction

The midwife shows them
The child's
Member.
If it were a girl, she wouldn't show a thing.
Not the very origin of the world.

The Turin Horse (03.01.1889)

His arms are still around the neck of that Turin horse.
Don't let go,
Friedrich.
What will happen to you,
What will happen to us
If you let go
Friedrich?
The wail of the superman
Flooded History,
And the last words of Zarathustra
Still float like buoys:
Mother, I am a fool!
The whip cracks
Above you,
Above the horse,
Above us all.

Psychogeography

Like the day your body
Learned to play dead
In the sea.
Remember, happiness.

The torch is yours
But the light is mine,
Said the darkness.
Remember, happiness?

Look, happiness:
Here come our people.
Trees move in the night,
Lurching,
Tatters of drunken clouds,
Stop-motion petroglyphs
Splash in the peat-bogs.
Remember, happiness?

Comical sparrows
Peck at the horse-dung.
We are dunnocks, stonechats, shrikes,
wheatears, wrens.
Remember, happiness?

Cursed, sad place,
Happiness.
Where we always settle,
Always set the stage.

The Origins of Literature

All night long the dogs howled
Because the wolf limped
Wilfully.

Gospel

But Judas was the only one who could make Jesus laugh,
As if the two of them shared
A secret.

Crumbs

Crumbs of words,
Spherical,
Polished
By fingers of silence
With the embodied precision
Of rosary beads
On the star chart
Of a waxed tablecloth.
Those crumbs
Can save hands.

Inuit

Silent Godthab woman
I can hear the purple pigment of your eyes
The thread of your whispers
That stitches a long, luminous and incomprehensible word
And blesses the kayak that pulls this needle
Through scraps of ice.

Antofagasta

For Xosé Luís Axeitos

If you fall get up again, you tell me.
Yes, get up again
I say,
But what if I fall
In Atacama
Like a tear
Falling
In the pure desert of Atacama,
Write an old letter
45 years later
To grasp why that tear appeared
That hollow piece of sky
That film of cloud.
I didn't want any trafficking
Of tears with fossils of tears
In this valley of tears
But what about this tear
Hidden in that
One
Stowaway tear
That falls right onto the title,
And makes a hole in Antofagasta,
Falls only to get up again
Along the whole length
Of that dry toponym
And weeps
Into the Antipodean hand
Of a sailor who has just written
Instructions
On how to repair the roof.

Forecast

The window
Looked out on the courtyard
And regarded wearily the other windows,
The cough of their somnambulist light,
The semaphore of dyslexic flags on the clothesline,
While a radio spoke of a storm,
A cyclogenesis, said the weatherman,
In the hope
Of whipping up excitement.
In the mirror
I found a pet
To protect.

Chess Repertoire

A silent repertoire
A mirror of water
Where you cannot see yourself.
You know there will be other things
When you've gone.
In the hollow space
Of your table-top
Foxgloves
Burst into laughter.
Cornflowers sprout
Along your bishop's diagonal.
Angelica roots
On the rook's shore-line.
How much
Would the jump of a knight's horse
Weigh on the Ohio Scales?

The Hunt

I'm on the hunt for a poem,
A creature that doesn't yet exist,
A neuropterous insect like indolence.
Something that takes me out of myself
Like a Spanish fear.
A poem that hides itself away
In the necrosis of the sacred chestnut tree.
A poem that will tie,
From the very first draft,
The laces of my shoes.

Whistle

To climb Teide
From the valley of Hope,
Walk through a sea of clouds
And then descend,
Like an apprentice lightning bolt,
On a whistle from La Gomera.

The Swallow

The incredulous Father,
The Old God,
Is holed up
In the place
He was born.
That crevice
Of clay
Among the clouds.
He hears with unease
His rebellious son's cry:
Why have you abandoned me?
But all
He has to hand
Is a swallow
To pluck out
The thorns.

Autobiography

For the Lapis em luta bookshop

Like a hare, I drank
the invisible ink of the night rain,
licking up the fat of the first light.
I am a poem.
I want to be free for one more day.

I know all about him,
The hunter.
I come from there, from his world,
Was raised in his shadow,
Grew wild
In his man-fear,
His man-faith,
His man-smell.

I don't know who I am,
Whether human or not.
Born of the air,
My warning call
Is the laughter of a stream.
I want to be free for one more day.

He has no idea who I am,
But he knows I exist.
He will make my life
his own reason for living.

Look at his footprint,
The greed of his hostile benevolence,
Capable of travelling to the Great Beyond
Just to ask for me.
Maybe he'll go mad
And burn

All the poems
That fled to a hidden land.

Better to slip inside his skin,
His man-fear,
His man-smell,
Live undercover
In his lair
One more day.

He doesn't know about the people
Who play in his body.
I hold the key to his inner life.
Lock myself in,
Poem,
Animal,
I want to be free one day more.

and III

FUNERAL ORATIONS

Un libro retoñaba de su cadáver muerto

A book sprouted from his dead body.

CÉSAR VALLEJO
(From *Spain, Take This Chalice From Me*)

The Mouth of the Earth

*To freedom's martyrs in the mass graves of Aranga,
on the banks of the river Mandeo.*

As the saying goes: The earth swallowed them up.
But I, who am the earth,
a small patch of earth,
a few metres of land
in-land,
what I feel is their hunger,
the teeth that seek
my nipples;
strands of roots,
pulp of time,
carrion of rotting hours,
the smoked weave of low cloud,
bread of darkness,
sour ferment of shadows
in the furrows of nails,
fragments of moon
in the abandoned centre of a glance.

More than anyone, perhaps,
I felt the fatal pre-empting,
these unquiet dead,
the echoing shout of the bullets' report.
They clung to me
with a last word
in their mouths,
that blade of grass,
that bramble,
the bone of elder tree.

I took care of their shoes,
their buttons,
their buckles,

their combs,
their pencils.
The little they had
a dowry for the rubble.

I didn't ask for this.
Neither did they.
They didn't choose
to fall into me.
But I am no grave.
I raised my people
underground
in the exile of my womb.
Tomb-like your tomb-country
where crime is rewarded,
paid for
in currency forged by forgetting.

The Gypsy Basketweavers

From Liáns there comes a sound.
Where, oh where?
Of feet that cannot touch the ground.
Where, oh where?
Of leaves falling down
in the mouth of a guitar.
Of children hungry for a blue mouthful
of fate, with outstretched arms.
Where, oh where?
Of angels who shout
through the bullet holes
of death, wrong way round.
Where, oh where?
Of leaves falling onto names,
sewing a coat of names,
bandaging the hands of names,
the wicker bones of names.

Where, oh where?
It's the first green shoot in the sally grove.
Where, oh where?
The way
The way to weave a basket, a hamper, a creel.

Where, oh where?
A whip of stolen wicker vibrates
with the whinnying sound of loss.

Where, oh where?
It's the rhythm of all the baskets bore.
Where, oh where?
The step of the mothers of every thing
gathering in
the first wicker rounds.

Fruit, sun, moon, mouth,
bread and dance.
The seed-bed of baskets.

Where, oh where?
Where is the branching absence,
the braided nest of a bird that was dreamed?
The way,
the way to weave a basket.
Antonio Camacho Montoya
Antonio Montoya Camacho
Manuel Jiménez Montoya
The way,
the way to weave a basket.
Jiménez Camacho Manuel Montoya Antonio Camacho
Jiménez Camacho Antonio Montoya Montoya Montoya
Jiménez Jiménez Camacho Camacho Camacho Antonio
Antonio Antonio Manuel Antonio
Camacho
Jiménez
Montoya

Where, oh where?
It cannot be.

Where, oh where?
It cannot be.
Where, oh where?
It can
not
be!

Invisibilem Tanquat Videns

The path of the righteous is like the morning sun,
shining ever brighter till the full light of day.

There goes Manuel Espiña;
His body is Proverb.

Let your eyes look directly forward,
and your gaze be straight before you.

At that point, Manuel says:
Listen here, Proverb!
And just a minute Solomon, son of David, King of Israel,
I have to take my eyes off the path.
I have to look at what's there
On the margins, in History's ditches.
I have to gather it all up:
The words that were cut short,
Crumbs of hope,
Shards of dawn.
His every step strays from the path.

Manuel likes to visit the ant,
He'd like Proverb to do what it does
And say what it says:
The ant has no master,
No King, no God!
But Manuel, that's not what the proverb says.
And how do you know?
Because Proverb is me, and you, and me.
Is that so? Well I just read it on a gravestone!
God likes that kind of graffiti.
I mean, he doesn't like to exist
Too much.

Now, Proverb didn't know what to say to that.
God likes that?
You never know with Espiña;
He's for the birds, really.
Well, I couldn't see him very well but I did hear him laugh.
Did you now? And what did it sound like?
Asks Proverb, dubious.
Like the fairy folk, says Manuel.
Like a lark in the free sky of History.
He can't help laughing himself
And turns suddenly
To look Proverb in the eye;
Can I tell you something, brother?
God's a bit on the short side!
Don't tell anyone but he's a bit of a squirt.
He's had a rough time of it, a tough time of it,
He's been through the mill.
And he has a weak chest.
Sometimes, at night, he's a window coughing,
A lamp the cold clings to,
A lame wolf that gnaws its own leg
Caught in a trap
Till he frees it.
And there are days
He needs someone to brush the flies from his face.
He needs protection.
But that's a secret just between us,
Manuel tells Proverbio.
It's our job to protect God.
He's titchy.
That's the mistake everyone makes.
They think of him as a Supreme Being.
Infinite,
Eternal,
Immune,
With impunity,
The Great Champion.

But I'm telling you, he's really puny.
Can't sleep at night because of the coughing,
Or he gets nightmares
Or he gets hungry,
And I mean sublimely hungry,
Or he's scared,
Or he has a pain,
Insurmountably scared,
Supreme pain.

Then his tone changed:
But you should hear him laugh!
That's something you'll never forget.
Fairy truth.
God's truth.

The Lovers

They had to flee,
flee from their own names,
grip them between their teeth
in the grottos of their gums
like the roots of some ancient tongue.

Flee,
they had to flee
from their bodies.
Carry them furtively
on the raft of a glance,
shielded by their eyelashes
while barefoot shepherd-boys
trod the sun's last rays.

Flee,
they had to flee
from History,
shift the great flagstone of the world
with their fingertips,
dress in dead hours
in the ocean's water-clock.

They had to flee.
Flee from the cradle
just to be born.
From words
to be able to speak.
Burn on the inside
with a mourning cold
so they could see themselves
in the demented depths
of mirrors.

Flee,
they had to flee
from love
just to love each other.

Atlantic Trench

What was Ánxel Vila made of?
Ánxel was made of water.
Except for his gold tooth
and the deep-sea optics of his glasses
he was all water.
We are all water with a thirst,
though everyone has a thirst of their own.
Ánxel Vila's water
was briney
like the sea's remembering.

Each drop of sea
condenses all life,
contains a genesis,
the mantic words
of the first woman,
that unnamed woman
with her necklace of shells,
seaweed for hair
spores for skin.
The woman who could read palms
and see in them the most wondrous estuary,
the reed-bed where flocks of mysteries splash,
marshes full of alchemy and awe,
a lightning-bolt that decapitates the dark,
the ferment of phosphorescence,
the moon that impregnates the clay,
the first ruckus,
drunken dream of matter
that swims and flies
gets up and falls,
falls,
straightens up
and staggers, blinks

because it has sea in its eyes,
the sea inside,
the sea outside,
a teardrop that laughs
and tints the gloom a cobalt blue.
No, we will not fall from the line of the horizon.

What was Ánxel Vila made of?
How many huge waves,
how many sunken ships,
how many skinned hands,
nights without sleep,
how many water clocks
regurgitating beats,
how much clamour in the void,
how much prayer and blasphemy,
how many north-westerlies and maydays?

What was Ánxel Vila made of?
How many currents,
How many migrations,
How many times cast adrift,
How many faded start charts,
How many lighthouses, caverns,
How much clinging fog,
How many globes, listing
Like breadcrumbs
On the tablecloth?

What was Ánxel Vila made of?
Of wood.
The best kind.
The kind of wood that speaks
like an Argonaut prow of oak.
You could see it in his body,
the way he and his boat
both moved.

And in the same way he freed thought,
he steered towards hidden land
just as souls do,
for they too are boats
and have known the beyond since childhood,
known how to stay afloat in a storm,
stitching the line of the horizon.

What was Ánxel Vila made of?
Of love.
That word they say we should take out of poems.
That's what it was.
He turned into a bit of a cockroach,
armoured, opaque as the sound of rigid wings.
Whatever.
Ánxel Vila was made of love.

A lot of love.
Love of his people, of his boat, of the sea.
Of nature's coming into consciousness.
Only a lover could map that route
through swamp infinity.
Only he could see into the invisible,
see the blinking light of hell on the radar.
He took us there
and brought us safely back.
For love.
That shadowy polyp,
that sea nettle
that stings from the skin in,
that creature,
love.

Allegro

One day, many years ago,
You spoke about the pupil in the water's eye.
You took me there,
It was in your eyes
At the dead centre of a lake in Cremona,
Where the luthier
Varnished his violin with primordial fog
And the soul of the wood
Was penetrated
By botanical imaginings
In the aquatic ferment
For a day and a night;
The breath of the drowned
Resounded in the rhythm of oars
Like ancient birds
In the counterpoint
Of flight.
That Argonaut movement
Of your hands
Was kept on course by the violin.
Allegro, my friend,
Molto allegro.
You led me over a bridge
From Juárez to El Paso,
Lightfooted, clandestine,
Memory's arms
Taking all the weight,
In one hand you held exile's suitcase
And in the other, an accordion
With the patched wineskin winds
Of the Odyssey.
Allegro, my friend,
Molto allegro.
You led me through snow

To the border with Finland,
Notes germinating
In the phosphorous' stuttering soul,
Marks in the ice
Of a pentagram
Cast off by the noise of History,
That stage where the spotlight crushed the sun.
Allegro, my friend.
Molto allegro.

Deer Blues

For B.B. King

The deer didn't budge
From the road sign
Till a car
Skidded round the curve
And the radio played
The thrill is gone
         The thrill is gone away,
            The thrill is gone, baby

Perfecto de Dios's Boots

He didn't want to die.
He fell into death through a crack,
Through every wound,
With a spurt of inflorescence.
He rallied all that remained of him as matter,
The ember of his shadow,
And stuffed it into his boots
To keep them alive,
A walking rhizome
Snug inside them.
And now,
The boots said,
We can rest as well as walk.

Singer and Minerva

Galicia stopped
Its exasperatingly
Slow sinking
To note the meeting
Of dressmaker María Miramontes'
Singer sewing machine
With publisher Ánxel Casal's
Minerva printing press.
The typographic composition
Of a wedding dress,
The painstaking stitching of a book,
Murdered.
Like the golden moment of a castaway,
My country.

Notes

Section I (Translator's notes)

p.26 *Monelos*
The Monelos river used to flow through the city of A Coruña [La Coruña in Castilian, traditionally Corunna in English], but is now channelled underground.

p.29 *Resurrection*
Mount Pindo is a granite peak of 627 metres in the province of A Coruña. It is rich in mythological associations.

p.30 *Soesto* is an 860-metre beach and nature reserve in the province of A Coruña.

p.31 *On Man de Deus*
Man de Deus is the name of a great rock in the shape of a hand on the stretch of the Galician coastline known as the Coast of Death.

p.35 *Traba* is a beach in the Laxe area of A Coruña.

p.38 *Sabucedo*
Over the first weekend of July in Sabucedo, in the province of Ponte-vedra, there is an annual round-up of wild horses known as the *rapa das bestas*.

p.40 *Situationist Rondel*
The Galician name for Sea Pink or Thrift (Armeria Pubigera) is *namora-deira* and in popular tradition is associated with love. It grows on the most rugged cliff-tops of Galicia.

Section III (Author's notes)

p.77 *The Gypsy Basketweavers*
They were murdered on the 30th September 1936. They came from the A Coruña area and were walking home with their wares at dusk when they were taken prisoner at the Pasaje bridge by a 'night brigade' who had failed to capture the quarry they were tracking that night. The bodies appeared in the Montrove area. They were all members of the same family. The eldest was called Antonio Camacho Montoya, 45 years old, married with eight children. His nephew, Antonio Montoya Camacho, was 16. Manuel Jiménez Montoya, the third victim, was 14. The crime

was never investigated. In the Register of Births, Deaths and Marriages in Oleiros the cause of death is recorded as 'meningeal haemorrhage, with dislocation of the brain tissue'. They are buried in the church of Santa Eulalia de Liáns, in Santa Cruz. Facing the church façade, the graves are on the left, and are now obscured by the leaves of banana trees. In a sense, they occupy a border. A limbo in the cemetery. They lie beside the graves of the innocents, the tiny graves of the stillborn. Of the angels. They were gypsies. They were, by profession, basket-weavers.

p.79 *Invisibilem Tanquat Videns*
For the priest, Manuel Espiña, founder of the 'Home Novo' community of the church of laughter.

p.82 *The Lovers*
For the two schoolmistresses from A Coruña, Marcela and Elisa (Mario) who were joined in marriage in 1901, and who, having fled their homeland, were reunited in Argentina.

p.84 *Atlantic Trench*
For Ánxel Vila, from Aguiño, skipper of the Xurelo and the 1981 expedition to denounce the dumping of nuclear waste in the Atlantic Trench off Fisterra. Following this protest, the International Maritime Organisation agreed to end the dumping of radioactive waste at sea.

p.87 *Allegro*
For Francisco Comesaña, who was born in exile in Havana in 1944 and studied in the Conservatories of Mexico City and Moscow. He was a maestro of the Stradivarius. He died in El Escorial in 2011.

p.90 *Perfecto de Dios's Boots*
Perfecto de Dios, an antifascist guerrilla fighter from Galicia, was killed in 1950 in Chaherrero (Ávila) while trying to get to France with his mother. He was nineteen.

p.91 *Singer and Minerva*
Prior to his assassination, Ánxel Casal was the founder of the Nós publishing house, the most renowned publisher in Galicia, and Republican Mayor of Santiago de Compostela. María Miramontes, dressmaker and designer by profession, supported the printing-house with her work. One of the last books published by Casal was Federico García Lorca's *Six Galician Poems*. The poet and his publisher were murdered the same night, 19 August 1936. María Miramontes died in exile in Buenos Aires.

Lightning Source UK Ltd.
Milton Keynes UK
UKHW041116120219
337017UK00001B/10/P

9 781848 616233